ADOLF EICHMANN

ADOLF EICHMANN

BEVERLY OSHIRO
AND RUTH SACHS

Published in 2016 by The Rosen Publishing Group, Inc.
29 East 21st Street, New York, NY 10010

Copyright © 2016 by The Rosen Publishing Group, Inc.

First Edition

Library of Congress Cataloging-in-Publication Data

Oshiro, Beverly.

Adolf Eichmann / Beverly Oshiro and Ruth Sachs. -- First edition.
     pages cm. -- (The Holocaust)
  Includes bibliographical references and index.
  ISBN 978-1-4994-6246-3 (library bound)
  1. Eichmann, Adolf, 1906-1962--Juvenile literature. 2. Nazis--Biogra-phy--Juvenile literature. 3. Holocaust, Jewish (1939-1945)--Juvenile liter-ature. 4. World War, 1939-1945--Atrocities--Juvenile literature. I. Sachs, Ruth. II. Title.
  DD247.E5O84 2015
  364.15'1092--dc23
  [B]
                         2015018817

Manufactured in China

CONTENTS

INTRODUCTION

Adolf Eichmann's involvement in the Nazi regime was not as a military leader or even as a soldier, but his role proved to be no less deadly. Eichmann, a small, seemingly unassuming bureaucrat, was responsible for ensuring the smooth running of the Nazi machine in its quest to eliminate all of those people they deemed unworthy. When Germany surrendered at the end of World War II, many high-ranking Nazi officials went into hiding, Eichmann among them. With the war over, their only hope of survival was to scatter to live in other countries with money they had put away. Eichmann, however, had spent the bribes he had gotten from Jewish people hoping to save their lives, and he left the country with nothing, not even false papers. He

Adolf Eichmann is shown here in his jail cell at Galami Prison.

managed to elude capture for fifteen years, but he could not hide forever. The British Army or Nokmim (also known as the Avengers) were determined to find all high-ranking people in the SS and bring them to justice. By then, Eichmann had relocated and, like many other Nazi officials, was hiding in Argentina. He had brought his entire family with him. He was living under the alias Ricardo Klement and had papers saying that he was an Italian national. However, his alias didn't hold.

One night after work, Eichmann got off the bus and was immediately captured and taken into a car and to a safehouse, where he was kept under guard. Days later, without most people knowing his whereabouts, not even his family, he was flown to Israel, also without the approval or knowledge of the Argentinian government. There, he was to stand trial. It was May 1960.

On April 11, 1961, Eichmann's trial began. By then, his family had been notified as to where he had been taken, and the world knew about his true identity and the circumstances of his capture. The world was watching to see what would happen. Shortly after 9 a.m. on December 11, 1961, the trial came to an end. Judge Moshe Landau convicted Adolf Eichmann of crimes against the Jewish people and against humanity. The trial had been hotly contested because of how Eichmann had been found and abducted and difficult to listen to because of the testimony he gave and the nonchalance with which he delivered it. He was kept behind bullet-proof glass to ensure that angry people watching the trial did not try to assassinate him before the end of the court proceedings.

Judge Landau delivered the verdict without drama or delay, stating, "Accused, the court convicts you of crimes against the Jewish people, crimes against humanity, a war crime, and membership in hostile organizations." The verdict itself came as no surprise to anyone in the courtroom. As a matter of fact, had the three judges acquitted Eichmann, there would likely have been an uproar among the spectators. The pale man in the bulletproof glass cage had angered so many people that everyone expected the judges to find him guilty.

Eichmann, who had stood at the request of Judge Landau, sat down heavily as the entire crowd watched in silence. Then the three judges read the entire judgment against Eichmann. Judge Landau went first, describing in general the atrocities that Eichmann had committed. Then the second judge, Benyamin Halevi, continued reading, responding to the challenges Dr. Robert Servatius, who was Eichmann's attorney, had made to the court. The third judge, Itzhak Raveh, then directed all of his comments to Eichmann's crimes. There was no doubt in the eyes of the court about whether Adolf Eichmann was guilty. It took the judges two full days to read the whole judgment against Eichmann.

CHAPTER ONE

IN HITLER'S HOMETOWN

Karl Adolf Otto Eichmann was born on March 19, 1906, to a middle-class family in Solingen, near Cologne, Germany. After the death of his mother, the Eichmann family moved to Linz, Austria, a city famous for specialty knives and high-quality steel items. It was also the hometown of Adolf Hitler. As an adult, Eichmann described Linz as being an area heavy with wheat. He spoke of the beauty of Traun Lake, and he also described a town called Gmunden, nestled in the cliffs of Traunstein, a mountain that he called the sentinel of the Alps.

Eichmann said that his childhood was glorious. He remembered mountain climbing and sitting in coffeehouses with his friends. They were days, he noted, of love, leisure, and life. He told the story of begging flowers from a certain Mr. Bugele for his girlfriend when he was young. However, people who knew him told a different story. Adolf's mother had died when he was a small boy. His father remarried. Some claim that Adolf was a slow learner. Others assumed that he had difficulty with his stepmother. But of the seven children in the Eichmann family, Adolf, the oldest, was the only one who did not graduate from high school.

Adolf resented being an outsider as well. His parents were Lutherans and remained in that church even after moving to all-Catholic Austria. With no separation of church and state, religion was a mandatory subject in German and Austrian public schools. If a family allowed their children to miss

Eichmann is shown here with his son Horst in Prague, circa 1942.

religious instruction, they were branded outcasts. But if the Eichmann children took the courses, they found their own faith subject to ridicule.

Adolf's family regularly attended a Lutheran church. It is therefore not surprising, and probably one of the few truthful things Eichmann said about his childhood, that a Jewish child named Harry Selbar was his best friend in school. But Adolf hated it when classmates taunted him about his "Jewish" appearance. His dark features pained him. "The little Jew," his schoolmates would call him. He found nothing funny in their mocking and teasing.

TRAUNSTEIN, A TOWN AT WAR

During World War I, Traunstein, which was located at the base of the Alps, housed a camp for more than one thousand civilian prisoners and POWs. After the war ended, the town was ravaged by the economic downturn. In 1933, the National Socialists gained power and began to persecute Jewish citizens. By 1938, all Jewish residents had been removed from the town. During World War II, a subcamp of the Dachau concentration camp was located in Traunstein. The town came under aerial bombardment several times beginning on November 11, 1944. Many parts of the town were turned to rubble. By May 3, 1945, the town surrendered.

AFTER WORLD WAR I

In the early 1920s, the German economy crashed. Germany and Austria found themselves trying to pay war reparations with money they did not have. These reparations were detailed in the Treaty of Versailles, which marked the end of World War I. The winning countries, France and England, declared that Germany had to pay the cost of fighting the war. When Germany could not pay, it started printing money as briskly as possible. Economists were not fooled by this scheme and adjusted the exchange rate as fast as Germany printed the new money. Before long, people were taking wheelbarrows of deutsche marks to the store to buy a single loaf of bread. Prices in stores changed hourly. When a company tried to pay its employees, the money it took out of the bank in the morning often could not cover even a single person's wages by lunchtime. People told tales of going into a restaurant to eat dinner and not being able to pay for a cup of coffee an hour later. They found it cheaper to use money as wallpaper since paper money could not buy wallpaper. This period of hyperinflation made money worthless and wiped out people's savings.

Adolf's father tried to put him through a technical school for engineers when his son dropped out of high school, but Adolf completed only two semesters. With the widespread economic crisis, it appeared for a time as though the young Eichmann would be a complete failure and an embarrassment

During the post–World War I economic crisis, old railway cars were sometimes used to house entire families.

to his solidly middle-class and well-respected family. When the senior Eichmann left his job at the trolley company to start his own mining business, he put his unlucky child to work for him. Adolf started at the bottom in his father's mining enterprise, as a common laborer and miner. Since class distinctions meant a great deal in Austria in the 1920s, his father eventually got Adolf a position as a salesclerk at the Upper Austrian Elektrobau Company.

Adolf Eichmann's reaction to this job was typical for him. Whenever he was bored, he lost interest in what he was doing. And being a salesclerk, tied to a desk, definitely bored him. He yearned for action. Once again, his family pulled strings for him. His stepmother was related by marriage to a wealthy Jewish family in Czechoslovakia. She convinced her cousin to act as a go-between for her stepson. At his trial in 1961, Eichmann proudly stated that the Vacuum Oil Company had offered him a contract as a traveling salesman, enabling him to leave behind his boring desk job. He neglected to mention that a certain Mr. Weiss, the general director of that American company, and a Jew, had been the one to extend such a generous offer to an unqualified young man.

In 1932, the Vacuum Oil Company transferred Eichmann to a desk job in Salzburg. Whereas before he had had a large region at his command, now he was again chained to a single place. His unhappiness grew. He saw himself stifled in a dead-end job and began to distance himself from the company. In an attempt to break out of his doldrums, Eichmann

Children wait for food at a streeet kitchen in post–World War I Germany.

considered joining a club of sophisticated men called Schlaraffia. This lodge was made up of middle and upper middle-class businessmen who simply wanted to get together to have a good time. They practiced refined humor and believed their purpose in life was to cultivate merriment and happiness.

Ernst Kaltenbrunner, the son of one of Adolf's father's friends, heard about Adolf's interest in this group. Kaltenbrunner, a serious and successful attorney, tried to talk him out of such nonsense. Kaltenbrunner offered Eichmann the choice between the "merry society" and the organization he himself had joined: the National Socialist Party. When Eichmann insisted that he could join both, Kaltenbrunner reminded him that the Schlaraffia lodge was a branch of the Freemasons. The National Socialists, or Nazis, would not allow Freemasons to be members.

Now Eichmann had to decide. Should he go after

wealth and position and hob-nob with these businessmen pranksters? Or should he link up with Kaltenbrunner and his Nazi gang? In the end, Adolf Eichmann did not have any choice. He was kicked out of Schlaraffia following a social blunder. He invited Franz Resl, a prominent writer and "chief cuckoo" of the group, out for a drink. As the most recent, youngest, and therefore lowest-ranking member, this was not his right. In 1961, he expressed no regrets for the way fate chose the Nazi Party for him. On the contrary, he used mythological language to describe how he viewed the National Socialists. They were gods. They performed heroic deeds. These gods were capable of manly death and also of fearless loyalty.

Eichmann and his new friends devoured the words of the Nazi newspaper, the *Volkischer Beobachter*. They read fiery words about national disgrace, betrayal,

This March 31, 1933, issue of *Volkischer Beobachter*, which translates to "The People's Observer," calls for a boycott of Jewish-owned businesses.

and the dagger that had been thrust in the back of the German people by pacifists, communists, and Jews. The Nazi Party promised a restoration of the glory of the German army and vowed to "damn unemployment to hell." This was the party that would forever end the shame of losing the war.

"Lord God, how these words gripped us, stirred our blood," Adolf Eichmann told his interrogator in Jerusalem thirty years later.

THE NATIONAL SOCIALIST PARTY

Adolf Eichmann officially joined the National Socialist Party in April 1932 as an *SS-Anwärter*, brought in by his friend Ernst Kaltenbrunner. He was twenty-six years old and had a steady girlfriend named Veronika. He had found a way to tolerate his job in Salzburg—he simply left every Friday to spend the weekend with his girlfriend, traveling sometimes to Bohemia, other times to Linz; any place but Salzburg. By November, he was accepted as a full SS member, appointed an *SS-Mann*, and he was assigned the number 45326.

Things were going well for him within the Nazi Party, but his job remained a problem. As with other jobs he had held, Eichmann was eventually fired. Eichmann contended that he was fired because of his membership in the Austrian

This 1945 photograph shows Ernst Kaltenbrunner in

Nazi Party. In early 1933, after Hitler came to power in Germany, the Austrians temporarily outlawed the National Socialist Party, however, Ernst Kaltenbrunner, the friend who had gotten him into the Nazi Party, continued working at his father's law firm without any issues. It is not likely that Eichmann's political affiliation had any effect on his firing. In all likelihood, it was Eichmann's need for excitement and his boredom with his work.

CHAPTER TWO

WORKING WITH THE NAZI PARTY AND THE SS

I n 1933, when the Nazis came to power in Germany, Eichmann applied to join the active-duty SS. He was enthusiastic at first, but once again, boredom swept over him before basic training was even completed. The life of a soldier did not suit Eichmann well. The repetition of tasks contributed to the boredom he so often felt, but a promotion as a result of completing a punishment drill well made him feel better about what he was doing. Later, Eichmann said that his success was because he had been angry at his father, who had refused to buy him gloves. Eichmann thought that if his hands froze off during the drill, it would serve his father right. After his promotion to *SS-Scharführer*, he was assigned an administrative job at the Dachau concentration camp.

At his trial in 1961, Eichmann claimed that he did not know that the views of the Nazi Party included anti-Semitism. He insisted that he joined for the adventure and because

Eichmann is shown here in his SS uniform.

of the betrayal of Versailles. He repeated over and over that he did not hate Jews, that his crimes were not crimes against the Jewish people. They were not even crimes at all but only the actions of a soldier doing what he was told to do. In fact, Eichmann was so firm about his lack of knowledge regarding the Nazi agenda that a few people at the trial were tempted to believe him.

Some reporters pointed to Eichmann's bad school record, as if to say, maybe he really did not read the signs and posters that singled out the Jews from the very beginning. More than one person was willing to give him the benefit of the doubt. A prestigious reporter named Hannah Arendt, who covered the trial for *The New Yorker* magazine, spent two pages explaining how he could have been naive early on, with no criminal intent.

By the time of his promotion, Hitler had been in power for eighteen months. The Nazis had organized a boycott of all Jewish stores. All political parties except for the National Social-ists had been banned. Plans were under way to sterilize gypsies and other minorities. Anti-Jewish speechmaking increased. Jews were barred from civil service jobs and all teaching positions, from preschool to university. Hitler preached publicly that Jews were subhuman. His platform included moves to deny German citizenship to all Jews, making them stateless and unprotected.

PROMOTIONS UP THE SS RANKS

In 1934, Eichmann requested transfer to the *Sicherheitspolizei*. This security police force had become a feared and powerful organization. In 1934, he was transferred to the headquarters of the *Sicherheitsdienst* in Berlin. They were also known as the SD, the security service of the SS. The SD had been founded by Heinrich Himmler the previous year. As Himmler's status grew within the Nazi Party, he handed over some of his duties to men he felt he could reasonably trust. One was Reinhard Heydrich, who had a career as a navy spy, took over the SD, reporting directly to Himmler. In the beginning, the SD was to collect information about other Nazi Party members so that Himmler could blackmail his competitors. The unit became so effective at this task that the SD eventually became responsible for all of the information gathering for the Nazis, including the Gestapo, the secret police. Here began Eichmann's true career

…lin, den 19.7.1937
Dessen Abschrift meiner … dem
SD-Hauptamt beigefügt ist.
Nachdem ich 5 Jahre Angehöriger
der Deutschösterreichischen Frontkämpfer-
vereinigung war, (damals antimarxistische
Kampforganisation) trat ich am
1.4.1932 in die NSDAP-Österreich
ein und bekam die Mitgliedsnummer
889.895. Zum gleichen Termin trat
ich in die S.S. ein, mit der Ausweis-
nummer 45.326. Anläßlich der
Inspektion der oberösterreichischen
Schutzstaffel durch den Reichsführer SS
im Jahre 1932, wurde ich vereidigt.
Am 1.8.1933 ging ich auf
Befehl des Gauleiters der N.S.D.A.P.-
Oberösterreich, Pg. Bollek, zwecks
militärischer Ausbildung in das
Lager Lechfeld. Am 29. Sept. 1933 wurde
ich zum SS-Verbindungsstab nach
Passau kommandiert und kam
nach Auflösung desselben am
29. Jänner 1934 zur österr. S.S. in das
Lager Dachau. Am 1. Oktober 1934 wurde
ich zur Dienstleistung in das S.D.-
Hauptamt kommandiert, woselbst
ich heute noch meinen Dienst versehe.
Adolf Eichmann
SS-Hauptscharf.

This is a copy of Eichmann's order to be appointed an SS officer.

as an administrator in the SS. He was promoted in 1935 and again in 1937 to *Hauptscharführer* and *SS-Untersturmführer*.

At his trial in 1961, Eichmann complained that becoming a member of the SD had been a huge mistake. He said he had wanted to be one of the men who stood on the running boards of cars that carried important people. He had seen pictures of them in the newspaper. Even assuming he was telling the truth in 1961, that he had confused the security service of the *Reichsführer* SS with the Reich security service, which provided these bodyguards, he did not complain when he started being promoted.

When Eichmann wrote about his early years in the SD, he filled page after page with trivial details about his breakfasts and his visits to barbershops, restaurants, bars, and coffeeshops. He complained about how inconvenient it was that he was not already married to Veronika because single officers had to bunk in barracks. After all this senseless detail, he finally described the job he was hired to do. Heydrich gave him a desk job, which he later described as "enough to make my bones vomit." He reported to a "good-for-nothing" student who happened to be curator of the Freemasons Museum in Berlin. This museum, however, did not honor the Freemasons. Rather, it tried to show how terrible they were. Eichmann cataloged countless seals and medals from various Masonic lodges, which appeared to him to be a demeaning clerical task.

Now he came to understand why the Nazis

Reinhard Heydrich was a German Nazi officer and chief of the Gestapo. He is pictured here in his SS uniform, 1941.

hated the Freemasons. Among the Freemasons, Jews and Christians mingled freely, without distinction, with their peculiar oaths and rituals binding them together. "You could not tell a Jew from a Christian over their glass of wine," he pointed out in 1961. This was not meant to be a good thing.

WORKING ON THE "JEWISH QUESTION"

Eichmann asked to be transferred from his desk job cataloging Masonic artifacts to the new and special department that dealt with the "Jewish question." At his trial, he insisted that the department was originally conceived by an SS officer named Leopold von Mildenstein, who was a liberal, tolerant man who wanted to solve the "Jewish question" only on a political level. Despite the weight of the evidence against him, Eichmann expected the judges to believe that he followed Mildenstein's example of treating Jews kindly, with great respect, and without the least bit of racism or religious persecution. Ironically, the use of Mildenstein as an example worked against Eichmann in his trial.

Eichmann maintained that once he joined the SD, he had no choices, that everything was forced upon him and he could only obey or be killed. Yet the very man he identified as his "first and greatest mentor and teacher" had quit the Jewish section and asked to be transferred to highway construction. Mildenstein was neither killed nor even demoted because of his request.

Eichmann finally married Veronika and now qualified for more money and better positions. Before finalizing their engagement, which had been unofficial for several years, he requested a thorough check of her racial background to ensure that he was marrying someone who was totally Aryan. He did show a bit of a stubborn streak when it came to the actual ceremony. The Nazi Party expected him to have a civil wedding, with old German traditions replaced by new National Socialist symbols. But he chose to have a Lutheran wedding in Passau. However, when it became clear that his continued membership in the Lutheran church prevented additional promotions, he left the church without hesitation.

Eichmann enthusiastically took on the work of the Jewish section. Under Mildenstein, he had been assigned to study Jewish orthodoxy. Before he left to work for Albert Speer's highway department, Mildenstein convinced Eichmann to read Theodor Herzl's book *Der Judenstaat* (The Jewish Nation), a Zionist, or Jewish, manifesto.

Adolf Eichmann had found his niche. Who else would read Zionist materials? The "Jewish question" filled a void and gave him something to do that no one else did. Eichmann tried to teach himself Hebrew and failed. He petitioned his superiors for tutoring, having found a rabbi who would be willing to work with him for the unbelievably generous sum of three marks an hour (a full dinner at

-2-

Vorläufig muss noch viel Rücksicht auf die Litzmann-
städter Behörden genommen werden.
Es sollen die lästigsten Juden herausgesucht werden.
Minsk und Riga sollen 50.000 bekommen.
Im Altreich muss bei der Auswahl der Juden überprüft
werden, ob nicht dieser oder jener Jude dabei ist, der
von hohen Reichsstellen protegiert wird, um keinen zu
grossen Anlauf von Schreiben wegen solcher Juden zu
erhalten.

Es soll keine Rüksicht auf Juden mit Kriegsauszeichnungen
genommen werden. Sofern ein Jude im Altreich eine Kriegs-
auszeichnung besitzt, treffen auf ihn die Einschränkungen
zu, die mit dem OKW. derzeit vereinbart werden sollten.
Diese Juden sollen auf keinen Fall etwa alle im Reich
behalten werden, sondern im Gegenteil im entsprechenden
Prozentsatz mit evakuiert werden.

In den nächsten Wochen sollen die 5.000 Juden aus Prag
nun evakuiert werden.
ⁿ-Brif. Nebe und Rasch könnten in die Lager für kommunisti-
sche Häftlinge im Operationsgebiet Juden mit hinein-
nehmen. Dies ist bereits nach Angabe von ⁿ-Stubaf. Eichmann eingeleitet.

Über die Möglichkeit der Ghettoisierung im Protektorat.
In Frage kommt nur ein etwas abgelegener Vorort (nie ein
Teil einer Innenstadt, das hat sich nicht bewährt), oder
ein kleines Dorf oder eine kleinere Stadt mit möglichst
geringer Industrie.
Die Zusammenziehung beginnt in den drei grossen Städten,
die verstreut auf dem Lande lebenden Juden werden zwangs-
weise hereingezogen.
Da es zweckmässiger ist wegen der Überwachung und Belie-
ferung mit Lebensmitteln usw., sollen nur zwei Ghettos

This is the third page of a letter describing the process of Jewish persecution.

a nice restaurant cost one and a half marks). While that request was denied, he did get permission to travel to Palestine to speak with Arab leaders about returning the Jews to that British-ruled country.

LEOPOLD VON MILDENSTEIN

Leopold von Mildenstein was born in Prague in 1902, as a member of Austrian nobility. He joined the Nazi Party in 1929 and received the membership number 106,678. Mildenstein was interested in Zionism, a nationalist and political movement that supported the reestablishment of a Jewish homeland. Zionism had grown in popularity after Hitler's rise to power. Mildenstein was tapped to write a propaganda piece about Jewish Palestine, which he agreed to do, under the condition that he be allowed to visit the country first. In 1933, he and his wife spent a month in Palestine, then he wrote several articles for *Der Angriff*, a Berlin newspaper. Mildenstein's idea that the answer to the Jewish problem lay in moving the Jews to a Jewish state in Palestine was accepted. But when the process of removing all Jews took too long, Mildenstein lost his status within the party. After his removal, warnings against a strong Jewish state began to circulate.

The idea behind the Palestine trip, to move Jews there, never panned out. The plan was eventually abandoned because it was taking too long to execute. But Eichmann's report bolstered his reputation as the Nazis' "Jewish expert." He was able to pick up enough street Yiddish to fool his colleagues. Oddly, as the noose began to tighten for Germany's Jews after the Nuremberg Laws were passed in 1935, prohibiting marriages and other unions between Jews and non-Jews, Eichmann began to float rumors that he had been born in Palestine. He had gained just enough knowledge of Jewish affairs to be useful to his superiors. He professed admiration for the Zionists, whom he recognized as "nationalists" and "idealists" like himself. (Their goal of removing Jews to a homeland beyond Europe appealed to the Nazis at this stage as well.) Eichmann immersed himself deeply in Zionist philosophy. He sought to master Jewish customs and traditions. This knowledge became the weapon that he would later use against the Jews with deadly effect.

CHAPTER THREE

THE GERMAN TAKEOVER OF AUSTRIA

In March 1938, German troops marched into Austria unopposed, claiming Austrians were happy that they were "coming home" to the Reich. Hitler had successfully annexed Austria and the Nazi National Socialist Party was no longer banned. Austria was even temporarily renamed Ostmark, or "eastern frontier." None of the world powers seriously challenged the military coup. A few American newspapers even saw the *Anschluss*, or annexation of Austria, as a positive development that would bring peace and stability to the region. A British travel guide from 1938 mentioned how delightful it was that travel between Germany and Austria had been made easier with the tearing down of the border between the two countries.

Eichmann had continued his rise through the SS ranks. He was now a second lieutenant. Considering he had not even finished high school, it was a considerable achievement. The Nazi takeover of Austria meant a significant

Nazi storm troopers and sympathetic Austrian gendarmes destroy barriers and allow more Nazi troops into Austria.

upward move for Eichmann. Four days after the German military took over, Eichmann arrived in Vienna. Suddenly, he was the official "Jewish expert," in charge of the Central Office for Jewish Emigration. Hitler's ominous speeches and threats now became policy. Germany and Austria had to be cleared of all Jews. Since Hitler's notion of providing Germany with sufficient *Lebensraum*, or living space, had been known from the beginning, Eichmann knew that he had found a role with room to grow. The more land Hitler conquered, the more Jews there were to expel.

JEWISH EMIGRATION FROM AUSTRIA

Eichmann ordered that high-ranking and wealthy Jews be released from the concentration camps where they had been kept. At this point, the concentration camps had not yet been made into extermination camps but served as enormous prisons to "concentrate" Jews and political prisoners for labor pools. They were not pleasant places, but they were not yet the killing factories they would later become.

When the prominent Jews returned to Vienna, Eichmann invited them to his office to calmly and rationally discuss the emigration situation. The Jews criticized the emigration system, pointing out that by the time a person went from one government office to the next to obtain the proper permissions, the original exit visa had already expired. Eichmann listened attentively and appointed these gentlemen as heads of Jewish councils.

Under Eichmann, all the Jewish institutions in Vienna were reopened. Synagogues were active again briefly. One Jewish leader recalled at the trial in Jerusalem that early in 1938, Eichmann called him and some of his colleagues to his office. He treated them as equals. They sat

Seen here are Polish Jews wearing the Star of David circa 1940 to 1944. This would be the fate of all Jews who were not initially given exit visas.

in his presence, surprised at such civility from a Nazi officer. However, his good mood did not last long. As soon as he had the necessary information, he turned it against the Viennese Jews.

Their complaints about the emigration process were entirely justified, he told them. He set up an assembly line. Anyone wishing to leave Austria had to bring all of his or her worldly possessions (or an inventory of them) to the emigration board. The applicant entered the room with his or her assets and left with only an exit visa and the small amount of currency required by other countries to allow entrance. Eichmann's office took everything from the Viennese Jews: property, bank accounts, and apartments. All in exchange for the privilege of leaving Austria. If the Viennese Jews were not successful in finding their foreign visas within the two weeks allowed, they were sent to Dachau.

After Eichmann began to taste success, he became unrecognizable to people who had known him. Gone were his polite manners. He liked to keep the Jews in his power guessing. One day he would be thoughtful, allowing a Jewish congregation to celebrate Yom Kippur. On the next day he might slam his swagger stick on the desk and threaten violence to the same people.

Around one hundred thousand Jews managed to leave Austria safely, with nothing but their lives. It did not take Eichmann and his staff long to recognize the gold mine they possessed as Jewish money and assets flowed directly to his office with almost no accounting of the amounts received.

Hitler's main objective was simply to get rid of all the Jews in Germany and in the annexed or occupied territories. It was unimportant whether the Nazi officers involved made themselves rich off the Jews they deported. As long as the goal was kept in mind of ridding greater Germany of Jews, Eichmann and his staff knew there would be no reckoning

RESISTANCE TO JEWISH DEPORTATION

The Nazis attempts to forcibly remove Jews from their homelands while stripping them of their possessions was met with some resistance.

In Poland, the crime of giving any help to a person of Jewish faith was punishable by death. However, more than six thousand rescuers were identified after the end of World War II. One of these, Irena Sendler, a nurse, smuggled about 2,500 children out of the Warsaw ghetto. There were several stories of resistance from Greece, one notable one from the island of Zakynthos, when a bishop and the mayor refused to hand over a list of the island's Jewish residents. A Brazilian diplomat in France issued hundreds of diplomatic visas to Jews, giving them free passage. Japanese consul general Chiune Sugihara also issued visas to Jews, in direct opposition to his government's foreign policy.

regarding confiscated property.

When Eichmann's superiors heard of his success at moving Jews out of Austria, his assembly line methods were copied in Berlin and Prague. In Prague, his methods proved very effective. In under six months, thirty-five thousand Jews had been forced to leave, handing over all they owned before their ships sailed.

THE WORLD AT WAR AGAIN

In September 1939, Germany invaded Poland. Twenty-four hours later, Eichmann's office became one of the busiest and most important places in the Nazi hierarchy. The number of Jews he had dealt with in Austria and Czechoslovakia now seemed ridiculously small. One hundred thousand Jews? There were more Jews than that in Warsaw alone. Eichmann had to figure out what to do with at least three million Jews.

German soldiers invade Poland in 1939 during the blitzkrieg offensive.

Eichmann's office had already begun to experience problems finding nations that would accept the Jews he did not want. The United States and Britain put strict quotas on Jewish immigration. Eichmann found it harder to motivate people to give him everything they owned if they knew in advance they would not be able to enter another country. And now there was the war to worry about. After Germany invaded Poland, Britain and France declared war on Germany. Ships that were headed to America had to turn back or risk being sunk.

The Central Office for Jewish Emigration became a section of the Gestapo dealing with religious enemies of the state, specifically Jews. After initial attempts at suppressing Freemasons and certain Catholic, Lutheran, and other religious groups, the National Socialists concentrated all their efforts on the Jews. Eichmann reported to Heinrich Müller, who reported to Reinhard Heydrich, who reported directly to Heinrich Himmler, who reported to Hitler himself.

Hitler and Himmler were still thinking in terms of simply removing Jews from Germany. Despite provocative speeches, Hitler knew that he could not afford to draw the United States into the war at such an early date. The Nazis had to maintain a positive image while they made their long-term plans.

At the 1936 Olympics in Berlin, Hitler had gone to great lengths to paint a cheerful picture of the

Hitler is shown here with Rudolf Hess and Prince Umberto of Savoy at the opening ceremonies for the eleventh Olympic Games in Berlin in 1936.

"Jewish question" in Germany. Jewish orchestras entertained international visitors. German orchestras played Mendelssohn, a Jewish composer who was otherwise banned. Hitler demonstrated to the world that Jews in Germany were separate but equal, which was an unspoken comparison to the situation of African Americans in the United States. Even three years later, in 1939, Hitler's public strategy had not changed. Eichmann spent a full year attempting to devise a solution for moving millions of Jews out of Europe without killing them. His first idea had already failed. The British would not allow Jews to settle in Palestine. Eichmann continued to pursue this policy, meeting with Jewish Zionists already living in Palestine. The plan faced opposition not only from the British, but also from the Arabs. The Grand Mufti of Jerusalem strongly supported Nazi goals for destroying all Jews, and he was not at all sympathetic to allowing millions of European Jews into the country.

Eichmann then tried to push forward a plan that had been discussed in Germany's foreign office before: emigration to Madagascar. He proposed to ship millions of Jews to this large island off East Africa and put them under the "protection" of Nazi overlords. In other words, his goal was to create the largest concentration camp ever known, with abundant slave labor at the Nazis' disposal. But Eichmann could never work past a gigantic problem. Germany was at war and needed all its ships for battle. Nothing could be released for other uses, even for such a "noble" cause as making Germany *Judenrein,* free of Jews. The ships would be out on the open seas, sitting targets for Allied bombers and submarines.

The Madagascar plan was never put into action. Hitler changed the rules of the game before Eichmann could finish his proposal. Someone observed anonymously, "The year Eichmann wasted on the Madagascar scheme was the most harmless he ever spent."

CHAPTER FOUR

THE PERSECUTION OF EUROPEAN JEWS

On June 22, 1941, Nazi Germany invaded the Soviet Union under the operation code named Operation Barbarossa. It was to be the largest German military operation of World War II. From then on, the war was fought on a grand and savage scale. Destroying the Soviet Union had been a core goal of the Nazis from early on. The German-Soviet non-aggression pact, signed on August 23, 1939, was little regarded by Hitler. The goal was to end the threat of communism and seize land within the Soviet borders for occupation by Germans. The brutality of the uniformed SS soldiers increased dramatically. The boycotts of Jewish businesses, the robbing of Jews by forcing them to leave the country, the firing of Jews from government positions, and the Nuremberg racial purity laws, and even *Kristallnacht*, the night in November 1938 when every Jewish synagogue in Germany and Austria was burned to the ground and Jewish businesses were vandalized, suddenly seemed like nothing compared to the violence that now erupted. For the Jews who still lived in Europe,

Hungarian Jews are shown here arriving at Auschwitz.

in the summer of 1941, their livelihoods, and even their lives were fraught with danger.

As the German army swept across Poland and into the Soviet Union, special units of SS troops called *Einsatzgruppen* (literally translated as "operation groups") followed the regular soldiers. The only task of the *Einsatzgruppen* was to kill all who were deemed a security threat to the German Reich. The definition of "security threat" was purposely left vague. In one form or another, it included members of the aristocracy, professionals like lawyers and doctors, clergy, high-ranking politicians, and people who acted suspiciously. And, of course, every single Jew was automatically put into the category of people who endangered the future of Germany and then murdered. The killings incorporated the method Eichmann used with Jews during the forced emigration scheme, for after the *Einsatzgruppen* murdered the Jews in a town, the SS claimed everything they owned as property of the German government.

There were only four of these special troop units, each with its own murderous commander. On January 3, 1946, Otto Ohlendorf, who was in charge of *Einsatzgruppen D*, described how the unit under his command executed Jews:

> *We orally instructed our troops to liquidate, to kill, Jews and Communists. Men, women, and children. All Jews were brought to one area and told they were to be relocated. They were transported to the place of execution in a wagon so they did not know what was happening to them. They were shot, standing or kneeling, with no outer*

garments, and their bodies were buried in trenches. Unit leaders had to make sure everyone was really dead. We took all their property, including clothes and watches.

The four units kept track of how many Jews they killed. It became a kind of game to see who could kill the most, with Eichmann as the score-keeper. All reports went through his office to be counted and added to a commander's record. As the Germans started to lose the war a few years later, the Nazis tried to destroy these reports and almost succeeded.

THE DECIMATION OF A PEOPLE

In less than a year, approximately three hundred thousand Jews had been shot and tossed into ditches. Since Jews in Eastern Europe did not always wear the Star of David, as Jews in Germany and Austria were required to do, the SS executioners could not be sure who was Jewish and who was not. That did not bother the SS. They decided they would shoot anyone who looked Jewish. By the end of the war, 1.4 million Jews had been murdered by the *Einsatzgruppen*.

At his trial in 1961, when the prosecution questioned Eichmann about the activities of the *Einsatzgruppen*, he claimed that the murders had

Heinrich Himmler was Reichsführer of the SS.

bothered him and that he went weak in the knees the one time he witnessed an actual execution. The prosecution reminded him of the many times he had made an attempt to be present when Germans killed Jews.

Eichmann had accompanied Heinrich Himmler to an execution in Minsk. The SS rounded up four hundred Jews and killed them as a demonstration of their skills for their two bosses. Eyewitnesses said that Himmler, a fat and well-dressed general, nearly fainted, but Eichmann barely flinched. In fact, one of the Jews to be murdered was a young man with blond hair and blue eyes. Himmler thought he looked Aryan and tried to save him, but the machine guns had already started firing, and the young man was killed.

From there, Eichmann drove to Lvov, where the butchery had already taken place. The bodies had been buried in a huge common grave with a thin layer of dirt spread over them. When Eichmann arrived, he said he saw blood spurting from the ground like geysers. That sight did bother him, he admitted later.

Himmler ordered that the SS find more "humane" ways for disposing of Jews. He was afraid of two things. First, as the war wore on, it would be harder to find men who could pick up a gun and kill someone at close range. Second, since he believed Germany would win the war, he did not want the streets filled with ex-soldiers who could kill so easily. It might be bad for German society.

By now, everyone knew that the Madagascar plan, or any other plan that involved shipping Jews out of Europe, had been abandoned. Long before the words "final solution" became part of the vocabulary, Himmler, Heydrich, Müller, and Eichmann knew that the only solution that counted was physical extermination.

EUTHANASIA

One of the first alternatives used by the Germans had been tested years before. In the 1930s, "useless eaters" were euthanized by carbon monoxide poisoning. Useless eaters included people with incurable diseases or mental illnesses—people who would not be able to earn a living and would have to depend on their families or society for support. The Germans had emptied church-run orphanages and various clinics, most of which were located in small towns. There were a few protests, among them one from the bishop of Cologne, and after a while the euthanasia program was discontinued.

Some scholars have written that the ending of the euthanasia program illustrated the effectiveness of protest within the Nazi government. Recently, as more documents from that time have become available, scholars have reached a different conclusion. The euthanasia program for useless eaters, they believe, proved two things. People in small towns did not protest or block the taking of residents from asylums and clinics, and the pastors of the local churches did nothing to prevent the kidnapping of these people. When no one lifted a finger to stop these murders, the Nazis assumed they were safe. If citizens of a small town would not rally to save the lives of people they were related to, then they certainly would not care if the Nazis came later and took away the Jews.

The euthanasia program also gave the Nazis experience with the use of various gases, especially carbon monoxide. By the time Himmler declared that another way had to be found, the executioners had become expert in building structures for gassing.

At first, Jews were loaded into mobile gas vans, large trucks with sealed compartments, with the exhaust from the engine fed into the sealed compartment. At Lublin, Eichmann personally tested a closed truck. The prisoners screamed, and Eichmann noted later that it bothered him. When he peeped through a

This is a mass grave found near Dachau circa 1949.

window in the cab and saw a hand grasping toward him for help, he said he wanted to get off. The driver assured him they were nearly finished. It is hard to know whether he was truly upset by the scene. If he was, he did not request a halt to the executions.

The SS briefly expanded on the use of carbon monoxide poisoning in large trucks. In a village called Treblinka, the SS built special cabins that fed carbon monoxide from a Russian submarine engine into the sealed spaces. Eichmann was given a grand tour and shown the latest technological advances in how to murder Jews.

Though 1941 was indeed the year that these atrocities began to take place on a large scale, the fulfillment of the Nazis' plans took another year or so. In July 1941, Hermann Göring, Hitler's second in command, told Heydrich, who told Eichmann, that Hitler wanted him to prepare a general plan of the material and financial measures necessary for carrying out the "Final Solution of the Jewish Question." The Göring memo has survived. At Göring's trial in Nuremberg after the war, the prosecution used it as hard evidence against him.

Oddly enough, Eichmann later claimed to a reporter that he wrote the memo that Göring gave to Heydrich. When he went to trial in 1961, his defense attorney said he was drunk when he bragged about his role in drafting the July 1941 letter. How deeply involved he was in top-level discussions will likely never be known. The rest of the paper trail has long since vanished.

STATISTICS ON JEWS KILLED DURING THE HOLOCAUST

An estimated total of 5,962,129 Jewish people were murdered during the Holocaust. They came from twenty-two countries. The worst hit was Poland, with three million estimated killed, about 91 percent of its Jewish population. Romania was also hard-hit with 287,000 losses and 84 percent of its population of Jews. Only one country, Bulgaria, had zero losses. By the end of the war, an estimated 63 percent of Jews living in Europe had been killed.

KILLING FACTORIES

There is certainly no question that Eichmann was involved in the infamous Wannsee Conference held in January 1942. It was at this meeting that the decision was made to go ahead with the systematic mass extermination of European Jews. Heydrich hosted the meeting. Eichmann acted as Heydrich's secretary, mailing invitations and coordinating arrangements. He claimed at his trial that he was a minor player at the conference. On the face of it, he would be right. Eichmann was the lowest-ranking Nazi in attendance.

Eichmann wrote Heydrich's opening address and kept the group focused as they discussed how best to carry out the details of the "Final Solution of the "Jewish Question." It appeared that no one even cared that Germany was fighting a war. Problems associated with troop movements or Allied bombings or keeping the soldiers fed and clothed were ignored. The whole focus of every officer and department was on the physical extermination of the Jews.

The Wannsee Conference did not change the methods of killing used. By January 1942, the carbon monoxide chambers at Treblinka had been shown to be far superior to shooting. Cleanup was also easier when the victims were gassed, and extracting anything of value from the corpses—hair, gold fillings in teeth—was easier, too.

What the officers at the conference discussed was how to make the killing more efficient, how to speed up the process, and how to move the Jews more

A US soldier stands in front of a German gas chamber in Dachau on April 29, 1945, when the camp was liberated.

quickly from one place to another. The Wannsee Conference could have been a business meeting at any major corporation. The questions involved were those of money and materials, such as: How can we spend less and kill more effectively? How can we keep supplies flowing at a steady rate so our factories are not idle? In this case, however, the factories produced dead people.

Once again, Eichmann found his niche. He was the perfect man for the job. He had proved that he was the most organized Nazi in the room. His efficiency astounded all who knew him. They knew they could count on him to keep the operation on track. And he, from years of meticulous research just for this occasion, knew the Jews, probably better than the rest of them did.

The Wannsee Conference was successful in unifying the Nazis around a common goal. For what was perhaps the first and last time in Nazi history, infighting was set aside as competitive military men agreed to work together. They put their resources at one another's disposal. Eichmann recalled later that he felt both exuberant and exhausted as the relatively short meeting, which had lasted only ninety minutes, came to a close. After everybody had lunch, Eichmann joined Müller and Heydrich for drinks and a smoke around the fireplace. He was proud that they did not talk shop that afternoon and only spent time together like men in a social club.

At his trial in 1961, Eichmann stated why the meeting held profound importance for him. He remembered thinking after everyone left, *It's not just me. Everyone feels this way toward the Jews. Every single one of my superiors ... they all want to take the lead in the Jewish question. What does it matter anymore what I think?* He described this as a "Pontius Pilate feeling," comparing himself to the Roman governor who absolved himself of guilt when he allowed Christ's crucifixion after the crowd called for Christ's death. He believed that from that moment on there could never be any guilt pinned on him. He was only following orders.

CHAPTER FIVE

DUTY TO COUNTRY

During his trial, Eichmann kept deferring the responsibility of what he did while at times seeming to be proud of his work. He had either convinced himself, or was pretending to be convinced, that he was not guilty of the deaths of the Jews because he had accepted the rationalizations of the Nazis and their new way of using language, which was specifically coded to eliminate any negative references. Himmler also understood that if his SS men had to kill so many people, he would have to make them talk in terms that would rationalize everything they did.

The SS men who had been selected for the *Einsatzgruppen* were taught to look at the murders as "awful things duty to my country demands." Murder was "granting a mercy death." Gas chambers at Treblinka, Auschwitz, and other extermination camps were renamed the Charitable Foundations for Institutional Care. Eichmann embraced all this, seemingly finding in these euphemisms a way to still his conscience. Eichmann's attorney, Dr. Servatius, would inadvertently demonstrate how widespread the use of such language had become in Nazi Germany. During the trial, he casually referred to "medical matters" when speaking of the gas chambers. Horrified, the judges asked for clarification, and Dr. Servatius repeated his statement deliberately.

As Eichmann's work began, he would ask that the Jews being shipped in the cattle cars to their deaths not experience any unnecessary hardships. When an aide told him that an entire trainload of Jews had arrived at one of the extermination camps dead from exposure to the bitter cold, Eichmann ordered that on the next shipment the women and children be allowed to ride in passenger cars, with only the men in the freight cars. He actually saw such acts as mercy, and expected others to recognize that he had tried to reduce people's suffering on their way to the gas chambers.

Eichmann did in fact take a real interest in the workings of Auschwitz, which was his favorite concentration camp. Commandant Rudolf Höss, in charge of Auschwitz, tried to pin numerous offenses on Eichmann at his trial in Nuremberg. It is from Höss's testimony that historians came to believe that Eichmann personally selected Zyklon B as the most effective gas, once the top brass

Nazi soldiers oversee Jews leaving via train to concentration camps.

recognized that carbon monoxide simply killed too slowly.

Eichmann very likely attended the meeting at which Zyklon B was chosen. He did meet often with Commandant Höss to coordinate their activities. And he did witness at least part of the extermination process. He most certainly helped Höss design the layout of parts of the camp. But Eichmann's role really revolved around the most critical element of the whole plan— rounding up the Jews and shipping them to the death factories in an orderly fashion. Eichmann's job was organizing transport. Murdering them fast enough was Höss's headache, not his. There is no record of

Rudolf Höss gives testimony at the Nuremberg Trial. He was later tried in Poland and executed in 1947.

Eichmann's response when Höss once complained that Eichmann was sending him more human freight than he could possibly kill.

As a master of logistics, Eichmann worked to set up a transportation grid that would have seemed unfeasible to anyone else. One of the first tasks required concentrating Jews in single locations. The idea of the Jewish ghetto had been around for a long time, but Eichmann modified it for his own purposes. In places like Lodz and

RUDOLF HÖSS

Höss joined the Nazi Party in 1922 and became an SS officer in 1934. From May 1940 to November 1943, he was in charge of the Auschwitz concentration camp and was its longest-serving commandant. Beginning in 1941, Höss began perfecting killing techniques. Daily operations at the camp saw two thousand prisoners arriving daily. Some would be sent to work, while those unsuitable for work were sent to gas chambers. Höss discussed his view of the efficiency with which he killed people, saying, "You could dispose of 2,000 head in half an hour, but it was the burning that took all the time. The killing was easy; you didn't even need guards to drive them into the chambers; they just went in expecting to take showers and, instead of water, we turned on poison gas. The whole thing went very quickly."

Warsaw, he evacuated the non-Jewish residents of relatively small neighborhoods and packed in the Jewish population. He used his familiarity with Jewish leaders to set up Jewish councils in these ghettos. He knew how to work on their weaknesses, promising one day that a certain group would be spared if they complied with this or that order or promising another day's delivery of a shipment of potatoes or carrots if they were compliant. He wanted lists of people's names and where they lived.

Eichmann was able to find corrupt Jews in some places, men who were willing to sell out their neighbors on the off chance that their own families would be saved. Almost without exception, however, once the rest of the Jews had been "relocated," these men and their families soon followed. Occasionally, Eichmann would choose a "favorite," someone who caught his fancy or whom he deemed cultured and spare him. Two of these men later faced the wrath of the Jewish community when their willingness to work with Eichmann was revealed. One was murdered and the other became an outcast.

One teenager who kept a diary in the Lodz ghetto once wrote excitedly about the surprising generosity of the Nazi bosses. As food dwindled and people grew weaker from starvation, the Nazis came in and built a trolley system. The little train ran from one end of the ghetto to the other.

The writer exclaimed that it made it so much easier to get to school and to the work he had to do, now that he did not have to slosh through mud. For a brief moment, the Jews in the Lodz ghetto believed that there was hope after all. The little trolley, however, was built so that the Nazis could move the weaker people to the train station and from there to the extermination camp.

Eichmann's enthusiasm manifested itself in his search for Jews, which took him to all the occupied countries. Heydrich wanted Europe combed of Jews from "east to west." The highest priority was given to the extermination of those Eastern European Jews who were less educated than their German or French counterparts.

A peculiar incident demonstrated just how irrational Nazi logic could be. At the time that Eichmann was scouring Europe for more Jews to massacre, the Romanians had decided to outdo the Nazis. Without adequate rail connections to the existing concentration camps, the Romanians built their own. In six months, the Romanians wiped out 300,000 of the 850,000 Romanian Jews before Eichmann got involved in the process. The SS complained about the brutality of the Romanians, feeling that the murders should have been carried out in a more civilized manner. They thought the excessive violence was out of order and wished to see it stopped.

Eichmann was alarmed at the reports and sent one of his top aides to assess the situation. The aide returned and told him that the Romanians were planning to send 110,000 Jews across the Bug

This is a Jewish cemetery in Terezin, in the Czech Republic.

River into two forests on the Russian side, where they would then liquidate them. Eichmann summoned high-ranking Nazis to his cause. He felt that the Romanians should not have been allowed to

disturb his orderly efforts to get rid of the Jews. In August 1941, Eichmann began negotiations to remove 200,000 Jews from Romania to the death camp in Lublin. To prevent the butchery the SS so disliked, the Romanians agreed that their Jews would be evacuated by German troops. Before the new plan could be carried out, however, the Romanians "sold" their Jews. For $1,300 a person, plus remaining assets, a Jew was allowed to emigrate to Palestine, illegally.

Theresienstadt, a ghetto in Czechoslovakia, was another oddity. Heydrich and Eichmann saw it as their showplace for the world. Here they would send Jews who were well known or had important connections in places like the United States, and here they would be treated well. It was the only ghetto that was directly under Eichmann's command. About fifty thousand of its residents ended up at Auschwitz. Theresienstadt is best remembered as the ghetto visited by the International Red Cross in 1945. The Nazis fooled Red Cross officials, who issued a positive report about the ghetto.

The ghettos, concentration camps, and railroads proved to be a very effective system for delivering Jews to various extermination camps. In Lodz, Poland, 160,000 Jews lived in an area smaller than three square miles. Eichmann deliberately sent 20,000 more people to that ghetto, knowingly overloading it over the protests of the ghetto's district commander. More than 120,000 Jews in the Lodz ghetto died of starvation. This made transport to the gas chambers unnecessary, saving the Reich the expense.

THE TIDE OF WAR CHANGES

On May 29, 1942, Czech partisans assassinated Reinhard Heydrich.

Hitler greets Dr. Emil Hacha at Reinhard Heydrich's funeral on June 9, 1942.

The Nazis then exacted vengeance for the assassination on the nearby Czech village of Lidice. They
torched the town and killed all the men on the spot.
Next, Eichmann arranged for the transportation of
the 302 women and children to the death camps.

Heydrich's death caused a change in the chain
of command. An old friend of Eichmann, Ernst
Kaltenbrunner, filled the position. Heydrich had
proved a more effective advocate for Eichmann,
who under Kaltenbrunner suffered a series of minor
setbacks. Among other things, while he had been
promoted to the rank of lieutenant colonel,
Eichmann never achieved his goal of making general. Even at his trial in 1961, when such regrets
worked against him, he bemoaned his unlucky fate
not to have been promoted to the rank he believed
he deserved.

Eichmann continued in his role as the Jewish
expert, but as the tide of war turned, his section
of the Gestapo lost some of its importance. Not
because killing Jews became less important, though.
If anything, Hitler stepped up the rates of execution
the closer the Germans came to defeat. He almost
seemed to have lost sight of the war he was fighting and concentrated solely on ridding Europe of all
Jews at whatever cost to Germany and its soldiers.
Eichmann's role diminished because it became
harder to kill Jews. With every Allied victory, access
to the ghettos and rail connections was further
cut off. Every Allied plane that bombed a train or
railroad track destroyed his means of transporting

Jews to the killing centers. And more SS units were needed to fight, making it difficult to find people to do the dirty work.

With a general's rank still in his mind's eye, Eichmann devised a new scheme to get rid of the Jews more quickly. He would offer to exchange one million Hungarian Jews for ten thousand trucks. Eichmann sent a Jewish leader named Joel Brand to central Turkey to attempt to negotiate the swap with the Allies. Brand was captured by the British and taken to Cairo, Egypt. He was thoroughly interrogated. Finally, Lord Mayne, British resident minister in the Middle East, dismissed Brand with the statement, "What should I do with one million Jews?"

Having failed at this mission, Eichmann returned to his role as exterminator. Himmler ordered the shipments to the death camps stopped in 1944, not out of mercy but because he wanted to start repairing the "damage" so that Allied troops would not uncover the extent of the massacres. He wanted to burn the bodies and fill in the mass graves, dismantle the extermination camps, and clean up as quickly as possible. Himmler saw this as the only way to avoid a death sentence after the war. Eichmann, for the first time in his life, purposely disobeyed orders. He rounded up another fifty thousand Hungarian Jews. With no trains available, he sent them on an eight-day death march.

Like the rest of the Nazi command, Eichmann spent the very last days of the war destroying as many documents as he could. He had been careful

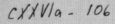

CXXVIa - 106

Der Chef der Sicherheitspolizei
und des SD

Berlin SW 11, den   9. März 19 42.

Auswärtiges Amt

D III 248.9

Eing. 10. MRZ 1942

Schnellbrief

Geheim

An das

Auswärtige Amt,
z.Hd. von Herrn Legationsrat **Rademacher**,

Berlin W 35,

Rauchstrasse 11.

Betrifft: Evakuierung von 1.000 Juden aus
Frankreich.

Bezug: Besprechung am 6.3.1942.

Es ist beabsichtigt, 1.000 Juden,
die anläßlich der am 17.12.1941 in Paris durch-
geführten Sühnemaßnahmen für die Anschläge auf
deutsche Wehrmachtsangehörige festgenommen wur-
den, in das Konzentrationslager Auschwitz (Ober-
schlesien) abzuschieben.

Es handelt sich durchwegs um Juden
französischer Staatsangehörigkeit bezw. staaten-
lose Juden.

Der Abtransport dieser 1.000 Juden,
die z.Zt. in einem Lager in Compiegne zusammen-
gefaßt sind, soll am 23.3.42 mit einem Sonderzug
erfolgen.

Ich wäre für eine Mitteilung, daß dort
keine Bedenken gegen die Durchführung der Aktion
bestehen, dankbar.

Im Auftrag:

261432

CENTRE de DOCUMENTATION
JUIVE CONTEMPORAINE

This document is concerning the process of deporting one thousand Jews from France to Auschwitz and was signed by Adolf Eichmann.

throughout his career to make sure that every order he gave could be traced to someone of higher rank, but in 1945 he attempted to purge his files of the smallest orders with his signature. He would have succeeded, but he had no control over the files of other Nazis, who were eager to prove their own innocence at Eichmann's expense. In the end, all of the rank and file of the SS had taken to the practice of covering their actions using the signed letters of their superiors. Their own words brought them down.

However, it wasn't Eichmann's written words that proved to be his downfall. Toward the end of the war when it was clear the Nazis were not going to win, he made the chilling confession that "I will leap into my grave laughing because the feeling that I have five million human beings on my conscience is for me a source of extraordinary satisfaction." For all his protestations that he was just following orders and was innocent or unaware of the true goals of the Nazi Party, when these words were quoted back to him at the trial, Eichmann could have denied saying them, but he did not.

CHAPTER SIX

BROUGHT TO JUSTICE

When Germany surrendered on May 7, 1945, high-ranking Nazi officials scattered in an attempt to escape trial and likely even death. Jews who had been held in concentration camps were released, ending a waking nightmare that had lasted years. One of these men was Simon Wiesenthal. Wiesenthal was severely malnourished. At six feet (two meters) tall, he weighed less than one hundred pounds (forty-five kilograms). A captain of the Jewish Brigade, a British army unit, asked Wiesenthal if he had ever heard of Adolf Eichmann. Wiesenthal had heard the name mentioned, but it meant nothing to him at the time, and he said so. The captain told him to look it up. By the end of the war, Wiesenthal had suffered horrors of both mind and body. His mother had been killed by the Nazis, and the Nazis had taken his wife. Though he was reunited with his wife by the end of the year, many of their family members had died in the camps. By Eichmann's own count, six million Jews had been killed in the extermination camps or by the *Einsatzgruppen*

Simon Wiesenthal is shown here in 1963 at the Jewish Documentation Center in Austria.

He felt that if he did not go after those responsible for the murder of so many Jews, he would not be able to live with himself. He sent a letter to the chief investigator of an American army war-crimes unit. He listed everything he knew about the twelve camps he had been held in, the names of the Nazis who had held him and others there, as well as the crimes they had committed. He was hired immediately to be part of a team that was dedicated to tracking down and prosecuting all former Nazis.

Wiesenthal captured a dozen SS members before he was transferred to the American Office of Strategic Services (OSS), based in Linz, Austria. But few knew who Eichmann was, or how important he was, and so he easily escaped the attention of the Allied soldiers who rounded up Nazi offenders.

An American unit did manage to capture Eichmann, but he used the alias of SS Lieutenant Otto Eckmann, as well as Corporal Adolf Barth to escape notice. Eventually, Eichmann slipped away from the POW camp and disappeared. No massive search ensued for the escaped prisoner. Eichmann continued to hide in Germany for five years. He worked as a lumberjack under yet another alias—Otto Henninger. In 1950, five years after World War II ended, he made contact with the still-existing underground movement of SS veterans, known by the acronym ODESSA. They took him through Austria to Italy, where a Franciscan priest—fully aware of Adolf Eichmann's

true identity—forged documents necessary for
Eichmann to obtain a humanitarian passport and
an Argentinian visa under the name Ricardo Kle-

EXTRANJERO

TUD DE CEDULA DE IDENTIDAD CIVIL

(LEY 5004)

1378538

This forged passport shows Eichmann using the alias Ricardo Klement.

ment. On July 14, 1950, he boarded a ship for Argentina. He worked for the next ten years at odd jobs in Buenos Aires.

At the International Nuremberg Tribunal after the war, when prominent Nazis were tried for their war crimes, Adolf Eichmann's name was mentioned several times. Commandant Höss of Auschwitz identified him as the Nazi bureaucrat in charge of the mass murder of the Jews, testimony supported by others. The international community added his name to the list of wanted criminals, yet it still took several more years before anyone understood how great his role had been.

Eichmann's family joined him two years after he arrived in Argentina, and his wife apparently never took on his new name. In fact, though Eich-

This was Eichmann's home in San Fernando, Argentina.

mann worked and lived under the Klement name, he almost flaunted his true identity. Argentina had been one of two havens for Nazi war criminals (the other was Egypt) that generally refused to extradite Nazis found to be living there.

When his fourth son was born in Argentina, the birth certificate had Eichmann as the child's family name. Veronika's Argentinian identity card showed her married name as Eichmann, even though their cover was that her husband's name was Ricardo Klement. Eichmann made a point of associating with former Nazis. And as the worldwide search for him gained in intensity, he seemed almost wistful for the fame that was passing him by. In 1955, a Dutch journalist and former SS man named Willem Sassen approached Eichmann about writing the story of his life. Eichmann not only consented but proofread the transcripts of the interview and noted corrections in the margins.

During the Sassen interview, Eichmann claimed personal responsibility for the most gruesome atrocities. He asserted that he formulated the Final Solution, that he chose Zyklon B as the poison gas for the death chambers, and that he worked with Göring on the July 1941 memo. Eichmann also provided chilling details. He and Sassen were thrilled and congratulated themselves on a job well done, believing that they would have a best seller.

Despite the openness of Eichmann's lifestyle in Argentina, none of the dedicated Nazi hunters could find him. Perhaps no one could believe that such a powerful and wealthy man could live in a primitive brick house with no electricity and no running water in a poor suburb of Buenos Aires, working at a desk job for Mercedes Benz.

CAPTURE

By 1947, the name Eichmann had come up several more times in Simon Wiesenthal's investigations. As he searched his files at the OSS headquarters, he found there was limited information on Eichmann, but that he topped a list of war criminals given to them by the Jewish Agency for Palestine. It stated that Eichmann had been a "high official of Gestapo headquarters, Department of Jewish Affairs." Wiesenthal became sure that this was someone who had been instrumental in running the extermination camps. Not long after, Wiesenthal was looking at the list of names again. He underscored Eichmann's for emphasis when the cleaning lady came in and noticed the name. She told Wiesenthal that Eichmann's parents lived on the same street as the office. Wiesenthal found and questioned Adolf Eichmann's father and demanded a photograph, but his father did not know where he was, he had not been in contact since the end of the war, and he had no photographs to give them.

An undercover investigation began, starting

with Eichmann's wife, who was still living in Germany at the time. She did not give up any information or indeed if she knew whether her husband was alive or dead. Then a major lead came from one of Eichmann's mistresses who produced a picture of him from a photo album. The undercover agent had gained her trust over several weeks, and finally got her to show him an album under the pretense that he was interested in photography. The next day, the album was seized and the photograph copied and distributed. Still, there was no further progress in locating him.

In late 1953, Simon Wiesenthal was talking to an Austrian man about stamps. The man showed him a recent letter but told him to look at what was inside the letter. The sender said, "There are some people here we both used to know," and added that he twice had to talk to "that awful swine Eichmann who commanded the Jews." The writer added that he lived near Buenos Aires and worked for a water company. Eichmann was once again on the radar of the Nazi hunters, but the leads fell cold again. It was one of Eichmann's sons, Nick, who would let the family's secret unravel. He was dating a young woman and didn't know that her family was part Jewish. One day he boasted that his father had been one of the high-ranking officials in the SS and that his name was Eichmann. Months later, when the young woman, Sylvia Hermann, and her father came across a newspaper article about Eichmann, they

WIESENTHAL'S SUFFERING

Before the Nazi occupancy in June 1941, Simon Wiesenthal, his wife, and his mother lived in Lvov, Poland. In November 1941, Jews were forced to do labor and Wiesenthal found himself at the Eastern Railway Repair works, painting swastikas and other symbols on train engines. Wiesenthal's mother was killed while he and his wife were away. He and his wife were later separated, and she was taken to other concentration camps for the duration of the war. Wiesenthal also moved to several camps throughout the war. Conditions were harsh. His toe was amputated after an accident at a quarry. He was forced to march despite his injury, and at the Mauthausen concentration camp, Wiesenthal lived on two hundred calories a day.

decided to investigate. They wrote to Fritz Bauer, the German prosecutor mentioned in the article. He sent them photographs of Eichmann that had been found over the years as well as some family details and descriptions. Hermann visited the Eichmann home to try to get some more details. By the end of the evening, she was certain that the man who called himself Nick's uncle was really his father, Adolf Eichmann. Now, it was only a matter of time before his capture. Israeli agents staked him out for months. Working undercover, they even approached him and asked for directions, photographing him and his house to be sure they had the right man.

In a daring kidnapping on May 11, 1960, they grabbed him in broad daylight on his way home from work. Two cars waited for his bus to arrive at his usual time, but that night, Eichmann was late getting home. The plan was about to fall apart when he finally alighted from the bus and was immediately captured and taken to a waiting car. Eichmann was compliant and actually signed a sworn statement saying that he was willing to stand trial. After several days, his wife contacted nearby hospitals to try to find her husband, but she never contacted the police. Hannah Arendt of *The New Yorker* noted a few years later that, as unbelievable as it seems, it is possible that Eichmann thought that if he was punished, German guilt would finally go away. He said this himself in a lengthy explanation to the court, and while no one accepted his words as true, Arendt wondered if he should be believed for once, an opinion that sparked major controversy that continues to this day.

STANDING TRIAL

International reaction to the capture of Eichmann and the way he was transportated to Israel was overwhelmingly negative. Even the United States ambassador to the United Nations, Henry Cabot Lodge, soundly denounced Israel's actions. He then brokered an agreement that resulted in an official apology to Argentina by Israel. Argentina in turn dropped its request that Israel return Eichmann.

Israel organized a special police department, Bureau 06, made up of German-speaking police officers, to investigate the case against Eichmann, as well as to ensure that he did not escape. The officers of Bureau 06 undertook an extensive interview of Eichmann. The transcript of these tapes filled more than 3,500 pages.

Dr. Robert Servatius, a German national and a friend of Eichmann's stepbrother, volunteered to represent Eichmann. Almost a year passed between Eichmann's arrest and the start of the trial, a year that was filled with unprecedented international cooperation in the opening of closed archives from the Nazi period.

Since the government of Israel knew that the whole world would be watching the Eichmann trial, great care was taken to make it a show trial, yet one that would be just and fair. It would also be the first televised trial in history. The judges, Moshe Landau, Benyamin Halevi, and Itzhak Raveh, had reputations as serious, thoughtful adjudicators. All three were German Jews; all three had escaped Germany in 1933.

The Israelis built a bulletproof glass cage for Adolf Eichmann to sit in throughout the trial. It was to protect him from survivors of the death camps

Adolf Eichmann stands in the bulletproof box that was used during his trial.

who might seek their own revenge, and it made it easier for the police to ensure that the SS underground did not make a rescue attempt or slip him cyanide.

The trial quickly became a very powerful emotional experience for the 750 observers allowed into the courtroom each day. In the more than fifteen years since the end of the war, the survivors of the extermination camps had kept quiet. Whereas German society had rebuilt and flaunted its wealth, survivors of Auschwitz and Treblinka, people who had lived through Sobibor and Bergen-Belsen, were ashamed to talk about what had happened to them. Now their stories would be told.

A few legal observers complained that

Eichmann's trial was not the right place for these survivors to speak. Even the judges became impatient with the prosecutor, Gideon Hausner, when yet another witness spoke of the gas chambers or wept as she described how her baby's skull had been crushed in front of her eyes. "What is the relevance of this with regards to Adolf Eichmann?" they asked.

Eichmann based his defense on two points. He had not personally killed a single person, and he was only following orders. Both points were rejected by the court. Höss may have, as Eichmann claimed, made the decision to use Zyklon B so that he could murder nine thousand Jews a day instead of two thousand. But Höss's decision would have been meaningless if Eichmann had not delivered the human freight. The judges ruled that a cattle car could be a murder weapon in the same way the gas chamber was. Both made up parts of a lethal arsenal that had been unleashed for the sole purpose of slaughtering as many Jews as possible.

After fourteen weeks of testimony, more than 1,500 documents reviewed, and one hundred witnesses giving testimony, the Eichmann trial had finally ended. On December 11, the judges announced their verdict. Eichmann was convicted on all counts. He then appealed to Israel's Supreme Court, but his appeal was rejected. On May 31, Israeli president Itzhak Ben-Zvi rejected his request for clemency. Adolf Eichmann refused a final meal

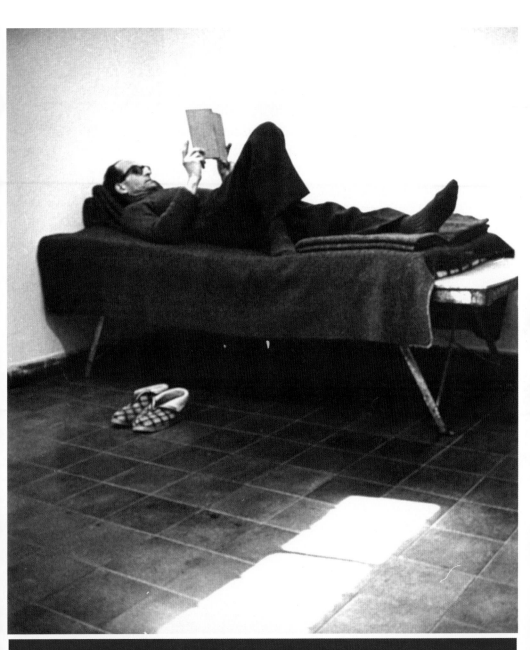

Eichmann is seen here lying in his cell.

but drank some Israeli wine and was hanged just a few minutes later, shortly after midnight on June 1, 1962, at Ramla prison, where he was being held. Two people simultaneously pulled the lever. His final words were, "After a while, gentlemen, we shall all meet again. Such is the fate of all men. Long live Germany, long live Argentina, long live Austria. I shall not forget them. I greet my wife, my family, and friends. I had to obey the rules of war and my flag. I am ready."

Shortly after his execution, Adolf Eichmann was cremated and his ashes were scattered at sea in international waters to ensure that there would be no place to create a memorial.

TIMELINE

1906 **March 19:** Adolf Eichman is born in
Solingen, Germany.

1914 Eichmann's family moves to Linz,
Austria.

1925 Eichmann works for the Electrical
Construction Company.

1927–32 Eichmann works for the Vacuum Oil
Company in Upper Austria.

1933 **January 30:** Adolf Hitler, Fuhrer of the
Nazi Party, is appointed chancellor of
Germany on.
Eichmann leaves Austria for Germany,
joins the Austrian Legion, and begins
military training.

1934 Eichmann, now a corporal in the SS, is
stationed at the concentration camp in
Dachau.

1937 Eichmann goes on an inspection tour of
Palestine to work on the "solution to the
Jewish problem."

1938 Hitler annexes Austria, and Eichmann is
transferred to Vienna and put in charge
of the Central Office for Jewish Emigration.
November 9–10: "The night of the bro-
ken glass," or *Kristallnacht,* occurs.

1939 **July 21:** Eichmann opens the Central Office for Jewish Emigration in Prague.
September 1: Germany invades Poland and World War II begins.
December: Reinhard Heydrich appoints Eichmann head of the Gestapo Section IV B4 of the Reich Main Security Office. This promotion puts him in charge of the implementation of the Final Solution.

1940 **April 30:** Lodz ghetto is formed.
July: Eichmann presents his Madagascar plan, proposing to relocate four million Jews to the island of Madagascar.
November 15: Warsaw ghetto is created.

1941 **March:** Eichmann becomes director of RSHA section IV B4 and plays a central role in the deportation of more than 1.5 million European Jews to killing centers. Eichmann visits Auschwitz, watches a gassing by carbon monoxide, and observes mass executions carried out by the *Einsatzgruppen*.
September 1: Jews are forced to wear a yellow Star of David.
November 9: Eichmann is promoted to lieutenant colonel in the SS.
November 24: The Theresienstadt ghetto is established and placed under Eichmann's control.

December 7: Japan attacks Pearl Harbor and the United States enters the war.

1942 **January 20:** Reinhard Heydrich presents plans to coordinate a Europe-wide "Final Solution of the Jewish Question." Eichmann attends the conference and prepares Heydrich's briefing papers.
May: Heydrich is assassinated.

1943 **January 30:** Ernst Kaltenbrunner succeeds Heydrich as Eichmann's commander.

1944 Germany occupies Hungary. Eichmann sets up commandos to implement the Final Solution.
August: Eichmann reports to Himmler that approximately six million European Jews have been exterminated.

1945 **May:** The Nazis surrender and Eichmann is arrested. He uses an assumed name and escapes to Germany.

1950 Eichmann flees to Argentina by way of Italy under the name Ricardo Klement.

1960 **May 11:** Israeli secret service captures Eichmann in Argentina and brings him to Jerusalem to stand trial.

1961 **April 11 – August 14:** Eichmann's trial is held in Israel.

1962 **June 1:** Eichmann is executed by hanging shortly after midnight.

1980 Congress authorizes the U.S. Holocaust

Memorial Museum as a permanent memorial.

1993 President Bill Clinton gives the keynote address at the museum's dedication.

2012 President Barack Obama uses the museum to announce the Atrocities Prevention Board, which will coordinate the U.S. response to genocide.

2015 Ninety-three-year-old Oskar Groening, the so-called Bookeeper of Auschwitz, faces three hundred thousand counts of accessory to murder in a German court.

GLOSSARY

Allies Also called the Allied Forces, in World War II were comprised of Great Britain, France, the United States, and the Soviet Union.

Anschluss The March 1938 annexation of Austria by Germany.

boycott An action in which one group of people refuses to buy anything or do business with people from another group.

deutsche marks Money used in Germany until 2002.

Einsatzgruppen The elite killing squads of the SS.

euthanasia Mercy killing in order to relieve pain and suffering.

expel To force a people to emigrate.

extradite To return a criminal to the country where he or she committed crimes and from which he or she had fled.

Gestapo Nazi secret police.

ghetto A sealed-off area in a city where Jews were forced to live.

hyperinflation An economic crisis in which money quickly loses value and becomes worthless.

manifesto A written statement that outlines the policies, or goals, of a group.

Masonic Relating to the Freemasons, a large secretive group of men.

Nuremberg Laws Laws enacted in September 1935

that legalized anti-Semitism, took away the civil rights of Jews, and made it illegal for Jews and Germans to intermarry.

reparations Payments made by countries or groups that lose wars to the victors.

Treaty of Versailles The treaty that ended World War I and forced Germany to pay reparations, effectively crippling the German economy.

Yiddish A German dialect spoken by German and eastern European Jews.

Zionism A movement founded by Theodor Herzl, which called for a return of all Jews to Palestine to establish a Jewish state.

Zyklon B A poison gas used by the Nazi extermination camps.

FOR MORE INFORMATION

Holocaust Teacher Resource Center
P.O. Box 6153
Newport News, VA 23606-6153
marknat@holocaust-trc.org
Website: www.holocaust-trc.org
This group is dedicated to combating prejudice and
    bigotry with documented facts about the Holo-
    caust.

Jewish Federations of Canada
UIA 315-4600 Bathurst St.
Toronto, Ontaria M2R 3V3
(416) 636-7655
info@jfcuia.org
Website: www.jewishcanada.org
Established in 1967, this group works in partnership
    with communities across Canada to strengthen
    Jewish life and raise funds for programs and ser-
    vices.

Jewish Virtual Library
(301) 565-3918
Website: www.jewishvirtuallibrary.org
A project of the American-Israeli Cooperative Enter-
    prise, the Jewish Virtual Library is a nonpartisan
    organization dedicated to strengthening the
    American-Israeli relationship. The library's goal is

to provide a vehicle for research and study concerning nonmilitary cooperation.

Museum of Tolerance
Simon Wiesenthal Plaza
9786 West Pico Boulevard
Los Angeles, CA 90035
(310) 553-8403
Website: www.museumoftolerance.com
The Museum of Tolerance is an educational facility and the only museum of its kind. It challenges visitors to understand the Holocaust and confront all forms of prejudice and discrimination in society.

UJA-Federation
130 East 59th Street
New York, NY 10022
(212) 980-1000
Website: www.ujafedny.org
UJA-Federation helps more than 4.5 million people a year with programs that strengthen community, provide aid to the elderly, and inspire a passion for Jewish life.

United States Holocaust Memorial Museum
100 Raoul Wallenberg Place SW
Washington, DC 20024-2126
(202) 488-0400
Website: www.ushmm.org
This living memorial to the Holocaust is dedicated to

inspiring citizens and world leaders to confront hatred, prevent genocide, and promote human dignity.

World Jewish Congress
4 Washington Street
Jerusalem
9418704
Israel
(972) 2-633-30-00
wjc@wjc.co.il
Website: www.worldjewishcongress.org
A nonpartisan international organization that represents Jewish communities and organizations in ten countries and advocates on their behalf.

WEBSITES

Because of the changing nature of Internet links, Rosen Publishing has developed an online list of websites related to the subject of this book. This site is updated regularly. Please use this link to access this list:

http://www.rosenlinks.com/HOLO/Eich

FOR FURTHER READING

Bartoletti, Susan Campbell. *The Boy Who Dared*. New York, NY: Scholastic, 2008.

Bartoletti, Susan Campbell. *Hitler Youth: Growing Up in Hitler's Shadow*. New York, NY: Scholastic, 2005.

Bascomb, Neal. *The Nazi Hunters: How a Team of Spies and Survivors Captured the World's Most Notorious Nazi*. New York, NY: Scholastic, 2013.

Boyne, John. *The Boy in the Striped Pajamas*. Oxford, UK: David Fickling Books, 2007.

Breslin, Kathryn. *For Such a Time*. Ada, MI: Bethany House Publishers, 2014.

Fitzgerald, Stephanie. *Children of the Holocaust*. Mankato, MN: Compass Point Books, 2011.

Frank, Anne. *The Diary of a Young Girl*. New York, NY: Doubleday, 1995.

Gruener, Ruth. *Prisoner B-3087*. New York, NY: Scholastic, 2013.

Leyson, Leon. *The Boy on the Wooden Box: How the Impossible Became Possible...on Schindler's List*. New York, NY: Atheneum, 2013.

Lipiner, Lucy. *Long Journey Home: A Young Girl's Memoir of Surviving the Holocaust*. Tuckerton, NJ: Usher Publishing, 2013.

Lowry, Lois. *Number the Stars*. New York, NY: Houghton Mifflin Harcourt, 2011.

Matas, Carol. *Daniel's Story*. New York, NY: Ingram, 2010.

Rappaport, Doreen. *Beyond Courage: The Untold Story of Jewish Resistance During the Holocaust.* Somerville, MA: Candlewick Press, 2012.

Rosen, R. D. *Such Good Girls: The Journey of the Holocaust's Hidden Child Survivors*. New York, NY: HarperCollins, 2014.

Roy, Jennifer. *Jars of Hope: How One Woman Helped Save 2,500 Children During the Holocaust*. North Mankato, MN: Capstone, 2015.

Schloss, Eva. *After Auschwitz: A Story of Heartbreak and Survival by the Stepsister of Anne Frank*. London, UK: Hodder & Stoughton Ltd., 2013.

Woolf, Alex. *Children of the Holocaust*. London, UK: Franklin Watts, 2015.

Wulffson, Don L. *Soldier X*. New York, NY: Penguin, 2003.

Zullo, Allan. *Escape: Children of the Holocaust.* New York, NY: Scholastic, 2011.

Zullo, Allan. *Survivors: True Stories of Children in the Holocaust*. New York, NY: Scholastic, 2005.

Zusak, Markus. *The Book Thief*. New York, NY: Alfred A. Knopf, 2007.

INDEX

L

Landau, Moshe, 8, 9, 91
Lutherans, Eichmann family
    as, 11, 12, 31

M

Madagascar, plan for Jewish
    emigration to, 46, 47,
    55
Mildenstein, Leopold von,
    30, 31, 33
Müller, Heinrich, 44, 55,
    62–63

N

National Socialists (Nazi
    Party), 20, 22, 25, 31,
    35, 44
    anti-Semitism of, 23
    appeal of, 20
    Eichmann's joining of, 17,
        18
    Eichmann's membership
        in, 20
    rise to power of, 12, 23
Nazi regime
    boycott of Jewish busi-
        nesses, 25
    Eichmann's role in, 6, 42
    goal of removing Jews,
        34, 46
    high-ranking officials of
        in hiding, 6, 8
    rise to power of, 23
    takeover of Austria, 35
Nuremberg Laws, 34, 48

O

ODESSA, 82
Ohlendorf, Otto, 50–51
Olympics, 1936 in Berlin,
    45–46
Operation Barbarossa, 48

P

Poland, German invasion of,
    42, 44
promotions, of Eichmann in
    SS, 23, 25, 26, 28, 30,
    31

R

Raveh, Itzhak, 9, 91
reparations, 13
Romania, extermination of
    Jews in, 71, 72–73

S

Sassen, Willem, 86
Schlaraffia, 16–17, 18
Servatius, Robert, 9, 65, 91
Sicherheitspolitzei (SD), 26,
    28, 30

ABOUT THE AUTHORS

Beverly Oshiro heard her grandfather's stories of what happened to their family in the Japanese internment camps during World War II. She became dedicated to human dignity and justice for all and works with groups who help those affected by war. This is her first book.

Ruth Sachs was challenged to consider the Holocaust by Frau Pieratt, her seventh-grade German teacher who showed grainy black-and-white movies about her father, a scientist who had participated in the July 1944 assassination attempt on Adolf Hitler. Sachs later traveled to Dachau with a student group. She has also written a novel about the White Rose resistance movement in Germany and speaks to youth groups and synagogues about Holocaust issues.

PHOTO CREDITS

Cover, pp. 16-17, 66-67 Hulton Archive/Getty Images; p. 5 Ryan Donnell/ Aurora//Getty Images; pp. 6-7 (background) Ingo JezierskiPhotographer's Choice/Getty Images; pp. 6-7 (inset) GPO/Hulton Archive/Getty Images; pp. 10, 23, 35, 48, 64, 80 Rolf E. Staerk/ Shutterstock.com; p. 11 Paul Popper/ Popperfoto/Getty Images; p. 14 Three Lions/Hulton Archive/Getty Images; pp. 18-19, 29, 32, 42-43, 53, 56-57, 74-75 ullstein bild/Getty Images; p. 21 Imagno/Hulton Archive/Getty Images; pp. 24, 78, 82-83, 92-93 Popperfoto/ Getty Images; pp. 26-27 Wikimedia/File:EichmannSSdoc.jpg; pp. 36-37 Evans/ Hulton Archive/Getty Images; pp. 38-39 Heritage Images/Hulton Archive/Getty Images; pp. 44-45 Mondadori/Getty Images; p. 49 Universal Images Group/ Getty Images; pp. 51, 84-85 Keystone/Hulton Archive/Getty Images; pp. 60-61 Eric Schwab/AFP/Getty Images; p. 68 Keystone-France/Gamma-Keystone/Getty Images; pp. 72-73 Wolfgang Kaehler/LightRocket/Getty Images; p. 81 Express/ Archive Photos/Getty Images; p. 95 Gjon Mili/The LIFE Picture Collection/Getty Images; interior pages background textures and graphics Aleksandr Bryliaev/ Shutterstock.com, kak2s/Shutterstock.com, argus/Shutterstock.com, Sfio Cracho/Shutterstock.com; back cover Ventura/Shutterstock.com.

Designer: Michael Moy; Editor: Tracey Baptiste;
Photo Researcher: Tracey Baptiste